I0425354

Table of Contents

Introduction

If you are thinking about becoming a taxi or private hire driver (also known as a minicab driver), I will share with you my inside tips and knowledge with a wealth of my best and most useful information which will be relevant whether you plan to work in England, Wales or Scotland or Northern Ireland. The information inside this book will be important to you if you have questions on how to become a private hire or taxi driver anywhere in the UK - Scotland, England, Wales or Northern Ireland (NI) in any of the big cities such as Bradford, Belfast, Bristol, Birmingham, Cardiff, Edinburgh, Havant, Hull, Glasgow, Liverpool, Leeds, London, Manchester, Wolverhampton or smaller towns.

In this book I will talk about everything from meters, insurance, working under a radio company, dealing with difficult passengers, health and safety considerations, accounting and tax, sharing my tips and experience to ensure you make sure you are prepared and not going in blind into this industry as I did. In this book, I plan to inform you of the real costs, hidden dangers, and pitfalls and give you the insider knowledge that took me years to gain to allow you to learn from my mistakes so you don't have to yourself.

By the end of this book, you will be more informed to be able to judge if this is going to be a money earner for you and I will share tips and recommended items to make your life easier if you choose to go ahead and get started in this industry.

Taxis vs Private Hire Cars

A good place to start will be the difference between a taxi and a private hire car. A taxi is licensed to pick up passengers from the street (something which a private hire car is not licensed to do). Picking up passengers from the street or at a taxi rank is known as 'public hire'. Private hire cars can only pick passengers up if the booking is pre-arranged through telephone or app, this is known as 'private hire'. Taxis, unlike private hire cars, can do both public hire and private hire. If you choose to drive a private hire vehicle, you will be limited to undertaking private hire (pre-booked fares) only.

When a private hire car picks up a passenger from the street that has not pre-booked the hire this is considered a contravention of the local councils licensing conditions. Breaking these conditions could lead to you as the driver, having your license suspended. It is therefore important that you must ensure all your passengers are pre-booked and you pick up the correct passenger if you choose to become a private hire driver.

If you drive a taxi you benefit from being able to pick up passengers from the street, and if you choose so, in addition, you can hire a radio from a local cab company to be able to pick up private hire journeys too.

It is up to you what type of license you choose to pursue. First and foremost you will need a full driving license. In some areas you may have to hold this for a minimum amount of time. Generally, in most areas a taxi license will be harder to acquire and you may have to undertake a topography test (a test of roads and places of interest in your local area). Many councils allow you to apply to become a private hire driver without the need to undertake such a test. You should be able to research requirements from your local councils licensing department online. Do not hesitate to phone them with any questions you may have. I recommend you phone them straight away to find out how long the application is expected to take for any license which you apply for.

Usually licensing is split into two distinct categories; the vehicle and then the driver. A 'private hires drivers license' will allow an individual to drive a licensed private hire car, a 'private hire car license' will license a vehicle for use.

Taxis can be purpose-built for taking passengers and many councils only let purpose-built taxis operate (a saloon car would not qualify in certain areas). The advantage of having a purpose-built vehicle gives more space and creates a distance between you the driver and your passenger, its harder for drunk passengers to interfere with your radio and turn up the volume for example.

Purpose built taxis are expensive to purchase new and in some areas, the taxi vehicle license will be sold privately for thousands of pounds (as local councils only hand out a certain amount with a waiting list that can be years long). Generally speaking and depending on your local area, getting a private hire car on the road is substantially easier than if you were to put a taxi on the road.

The Radio

Unless you are in a position where you have someone to control where cars are and man telephones, you will need to hire a 'radio' from a local company. The radio is either a traditional radio or more commonly lately a mobile phone with an app which allows the controller at the radio firm to communicate and send you hires remotely.

Radio hire costs in the region of £100 per week, sometimes higher in big cities. It is important to consider that these private hire companies want this £100 fee a week from you no matter what your circumstances are if you are on holiday or in the hospital most companies simply don't care about anything other than getting this money from you. If you refuse to pay they will simply stop your ability to work, and you will stop earning money. It is important to research how many private hire companies work in your local area and try your best to get your foot in the door with a good one. Some companies have a waiting list for radios which can last weeks to months. It is important before you financially invest you make sure you will have a guaranteed source of income.

When you work as a private hire driver and rent a radio from a company, you will be considered self-employed but be prepared to be treated as if you were an employee of the company. You may have certain rules to follow. Be wary that some companies 'feed' some drivers (giving company owned vehicles more/better jobs in order that the company car earns more than privately owned vehicles on that 'system').

If you choose to drive a taxi, you can drive about looking for fares, wait at a rank or as an addition you could have a radio. It will be up to you to decide if getting tied into spending the extra £100 per week will benefit you.

Usually, the radio hire is going to be your biggest expense week to week and it is in your best interests to work for a company that is busy. Speak to your family and friends, colleagues and people in your town and ask them which company they use. The company with the best customer service and reputation would be my first choice when it comes to hiring a radio.

Business models

There are two types of drivers in the private hire and taxi world. Those that license and own their car, and those that drive for somebody else.

If you choose to drive your own car, you will keep all your takings yourself, yet be responsible for paying all the bills and maintenance costs. If you drive for someone else your radio hire, car and insurance costs will be covered by the owner of the vehicle. Working for somebody else the usual business model is as follows; you will need to give 50% percent of your takings to the owner of the vehicle and contribute for half of the fuel.

If you drive your own vehicle, you will be free to choose what shifts to work, if you want to do school or corporate work (where you will be tied into picking up passengers at a certain time on a daily basis). If you drive for someone else you may not be the only driver of that vehicle and may only be able to work certain shifts that may or may not suit your lifestyle.

Working for somebody else gives you some benefits when you first start if you are sitting on the fence, you can work out takings and if you think fully investing in this business will be profitable and may be suited better to part-time drivers with the ability to walk away quickly if things aren't working out. Working for yourself is a good option if you are able to work on a high earning system and will be working many long hours per week.

Some companies offer the driver the opportunity to rent a licensed fleet car with the radio included which can range in price. I personally tried this option whilst waiting for a private hire car test and was paying £240 per week for car and radio money combined which gave me a huge expenditure of £960 per month before I made any profit, that's not taking into consideration fuel expenditure too.

Start-Up Costs

Next, I am going to talk about some real-world costs now that you understand some of the basic principles. It is imperative that you factor the costs of everything into a spreadsheet to keep an eye on how much is coming in and out. Make sure you keep any receipts for fuel, items you purchase in relation to your business for record keeping and tax purposes. I find it is best to keep a weekly spreadsheet and save it on your computer, printing off a copy to be kept with your weekly receipts somewhere safe.

Here are some of the common expenses for you to list and take into consideration:

- Insurance: premiums vary in price and are generally higher than normal car insurance (you need to obtain a quote for specialist private hire or public hire insurance).
  Private hire drivers/cars licensing fee: variable cost per local council.

- Radio fees: estimated £400 p/m

- Fuel cost: variable. I spent roughly £20 per day with a 1.6l diesel estate car.

- Running costs and repairs: Servicing and maintaining your car and driving sensibly can avoid spending too much.

- Smartphone and sat nav: you can use a phone with a navigational app, a sat nav is always a good back up option.

- Taximeter: The taximeter will need to installed and set to your council's local fare tariff professionally. There are a few different options and they can be picked up cheaply from internet auction sites second hand or bought new.

- Coin dispenser: less than £10 online.

- Stationary (pens, a notebook or calendar to record earnings and a duplicate book for recording any card transactions).

- A torch: buy a torch which is powerful enough to light the front of a house to read the numbers in low light.

- Washing and cleaning costs

You may need to pay for an additional council ran course and an additional disclosure certificate should you choose to participate in school run work.

You need to take into consideration when driving that your livelihood depends on your car being on the road. If you are involved in a road traffic collision and your car goes off the road, you will have no income for the period of time repairs or a replacement vehicle can be obtained.

The Taxi Examination

If you apply for a vehicle license, you will have to present your vehicle for a test at a council location where generally your car will receive a very thorough and strict MOT. The vehicle will have to be immaculate condition and it is possible to fail for the most minuscule reasons. It is very important to arrive at the test center as punctually, polite and professional as possible as your car can be failed with ease if you end up upsetting your tester.

Giving your vehicle a wash is not enough, this is the most stringent MOT and cleanliness inspection that your car will receive and involves the tester checking everything on your car making sure your car is completely roadworthy and the paintwork is in good condition and small scratches waxed out. The interior will need to look as good as new so it is important to valet the inside, outside and engine bay also paying attention to under the seats and even cleaning the spare wheel and its compartment! They check everywhere!

As a minimum, you should service your vehicle before going for a taxi test, say a couple of weeks in advance to be aware of any problems and give time for parts to arrive and work to be carried out. The underside of the vehicle will usually need steam cleaned for most councils inspections with the car in showroom condition. I have personally had a car fail a test for dirty windows from driving through to the test centre so take a small cleaning kit to use when you park up on the day of your test to make sure it is very clean and presentable.

Many valeting companies offer a taxi valet service which should include steam cleaning the underside, cleaning the engine bay and a full exterior and interior valet, even dying carpets back to black if they have faded. This service usually costs in the region of £100.

Upon your taxi or private hire car successfully passing it's test, you will be issued with some plates to fit to your vehicle. Come prepared with a screwdriver and any other tools or items you may need to fit the plates onto your vehicle.

Picking up Fares

When someone phones a taxi company requiring transportation, the person taking the phone call and making the booking will usually provide you with the following information: the name of the customer, the pickup point, the drop off point and perhaps the customers mobile phone number.

When you arrive at the destination, phone your customer if you have been provided their telephone number as many people will not notice a text message. Make sure you phone them with your phone number withheld if not using a company provided telephone system otherwise you could be subjected to some unwanted calls and messages. Phoning your customer on arrival makes sure they are aware that you are here ready to collect them ASAP as you will not be paid for sitting about. I generally waited a maximum of 4.5 mins then drove off to the next potential fare if I received no response. Always double check that you are in the right location.

It is a sad fact that some people will phone multiple taxi companies at once in order to get a taxi as quickly as possible or just change their mind/get too drunk. If your passenger does not turn up this is referred to as a 'no show'.

Most customers you will transport will just want to get from A to B with no fuss. Be professional, polite and friendly which will increase your tips. You ideally want to engage in pleasant conversation while maintaining a professional boundary. You can gauge early on if a customer wants to talk to you or not by asking them in a friendly manner how they are. Every customer is everyone is different, some will want to tell you their life story, others will not want to engage in conversation at all.

Always confirm the destination as sometimes there can be booking errors. Always try to pick up and drop off your customers on the non traffic side of the road and remind your customers to check for hazards when exiting your cab. It's always a good idea to check the seats after they have left for any items that may have been dropped. You can buy signage to encourage the use of seat belts, many passengers wrongly assume that they don't need to wear one. It's best to encourage the use of seatbelts as the last thing you want is for someone to become seriously injured or die in your cab in the event of an accident.

If you are driving a private hire car, you will be unable to pick up customers from the street without the booking being pre arranged. You may come across people that come up to your window, asking you how to get a cab and if you will take them on board. You must make sure as a private hire driver that the booking is pre arranged. You can get the customer to phone the dispatcher and book in to be picked up, making sure you are covered and meeting the requirements for a 'pre booked hire'. If you are ever falsely accused of 'plying for hire', you can use a print off sheet as evidence that the booking was made by the customer prior to pick up.

Taxi Drivers will wait for periods of time at a taxi rank. You need to optimise what rank you sit in at what time depending on your local area. Find out where the taxi ranks are in your area and identify ranks near places that will be busy. You may want to start out in the morning at a train station to catch commuters, move on to the supermarket nearer lunch time and near the pubs and clubs later in the evening for example.

Occasionally you may encounter some undesirable passengers which will be covered in the next chapter on safety.

Safety

When arriving at the pickup point, always park in a manner which allows you to drive off safely with the doors kept locked and the windows down just a touch to allow conversation until you confirm that you have the right passenger and they are in a fit state to travel. Keeping the doors locked and windows just open a crack is especially important when working at night as people that are not your passengers and are desperate for a cab may get confrontational, try to get inside or spit on you and reduces the chances of you becoming a target for robbery. I always considered my safety 24/7 and being cautious has certainly paid off for me. I've been parked up having a break when a drunk tried to jump in my car at 12 noon drunk on a Sunday, you just never know.

Always look at the condition of the passenger(s) trying to get into your vehicle - for example, if they are staggering and covered in vomit, drive off without having a conversation with them. You can phone the controller later to explain the situation without getting assaulted or your car kicked etc if you attempted to politely decline them a trip.

Avoid confrontation with difficult passengers, if they are under the influence and ranting about a subject without threatening you, I found it best to answer with things like "yeah, okay, ah I see" in order not to cause argument. There will be times where you may have to refuse to drive to a takeaway late at night for example as you don't want fast food all over your seats. In such an instance you just need to be assertive, polite and tactful in your responses. If you are ever in the position that you get attacked, make sure you call for help as soon as possible and try to get away from the danger. Some companies install a panic alarm button which alerts nearby drivers, I would always endeavour to call the police in such an instance as soon as practicable.

If someone runs off without paying you its best just to avoid confrontation, how do you know they aren't carrying a knife for example? You don't want to lose your license if you got into an altercation. It is best to have a dash cam or CCTV camera installed in your car to protect yourself from false allegations and the footage can be used as evidence in the event of an incident or accident.

If you pick up a passenger you are not sure about and they ask you gauging questions trying to figure out how much money you have earned such as "how long have you been out for?" respond with "I'm just out". It's better to be on the side of caution than to fall victim to a robbery. It's best to keep a float of about £15, hiding the bulk of your takings somewhere in your vehicle out of passenger reach. Do not flash large amounts of cash to people. Anything of value you have, keep it as far out of reach from your passengers as possible, like your float money, mobile phone or sat nav.

Now the more worrying aspects about the job have been covered its time to move on to the next chapter; Preparing Your Vehicle.

Preparing Your Vehicle

You want to be able to prepare your vehicle fully in order that you can be operational and earning fares for the maximum amount of time you are out on the road. To do this it is best to prepare for some of the common hiccups you may encounter.

As well as keeping your vehicle serviceable, it is important in my opinion to drive with suitable tires for the season that you are driving in. It is a smart idea to use winter tyres when the temperature falls below 7 degrees Celsius as they have softer rubber and provide far better grip than summer tyres in colder conditions. When you drive all year round the last thing you want to do is have an accident which could have been avoided and takes away your ability to work!

Next, I am going to talk about some items that I recommend you keep inside your cab. I recommend storing spare bulbs inside your glovebox. I personally keep my headlights running at all times to improve my visibility to other road users. If you go to a local motor or DIY store you should be able to buy some reflective tape, it's a great idea to use this around the inside of all doors of the cab. People will leave doors open and do things like exit your cab without looking for oncoming traffic (it could be that extra little bit of visibility needed to stop a nasty accident from happening).

With doing so many miles on the road, getting punctures is inevitable. You can decrease your turn around time by keeping a tyre inflator stored in your cab which will save you having to change a tyre by the roadside or the time and cost of being towed to a garage. You can also buy a battery jump pack if you encounter a flat battery on a cold winters morning or forget that you leave your lights running. All these items that I recommend can be expensive, the convenience of fixing your own problems without paying someone else will pay dividends if you do your preparation.

You can choose to purchase break down cover or just pay for recovery as it happens in the event of a breakdown. It will be up to you to weigh up if a policy will be worth paying. Be aware that you may need to get a business policy which may incur additional expense.

When I was working as a private hire driver in Scotland, I came across a lot of passengers that did not have my standards of personal hygiene. You will encounter people that smell bad and if you refuse the fare, ultimately you will miss out on potential takings. Wind deflectors are great for getting a constant intake of fresh air and make transporting these people bearable. Drunk people can have a tendency to vomit and I recommend that you carry a cleaning kit, air freshener and disposable gloves for dealing with any spillages or sickness as fast as you can and get back out on the road. It is best to fit waterproof seat covers on top of the original upholstery to protect from cuts and spillages and this will help to decrease your turn around time to get your cab back to being clean should anything dirty the seats. It's also a good idea to fit rubber floor mats that you can quickly jet wash clean.

Unnecessary Spending

One thing to look out for in the profession is unnecessary spending. If you are making a good amount a day, and getting paid in cash it can be tempting to spend this money out of convenience in places like service stations. It is very easy to spend in the region of £10 per day, possibly more by the time you have bought lunch and few coffees in the duration of your shift. You can save a lot of money if you prepare packed lunches and have a flask of tea or coffee to drink from. If you work a five day week and spent £10 per day on food and drink - that's a whopping £2400 per year. The same applies to other things like paying for cleaning services. Try to save money where you can and record any expenses you have. You may be surprised how the little things add up and you can make an action plan to reduce your spending.

Zones

Most companies use apps now which plot the position of the driver inside a zone. A zone is an area of the map where any other taxis that are working for the same company as you will queue in for jobs. When you move into a zone you will automatically become the last car in that zone. If you were to drive into the zone area of Edinburgh Airport for example when two available cabs were already in that area, you may see the screen on your device say Edinburgh Airport 3 of 3. This means you are third in the queue in that area to get a job and will have to wait for the two cabs in front of you do be dispatched to a job to move up in the zone's queue. If a job comes in that is out of the zone, the closest car to the job is usually the one to be dispatched.

If you work in a company where zone areas are implemented you will pick up jobs in that area as long as the zone is moving and has a good customer base. If you are in a quieter area sometimes its a good idea to move back to a busy zone, or when in the busy zone position yourself on the edge closest to an area that's maybe outwit your zone which could be a nearby supermarket, industrial estate, hospital or airport where you are likely to pick up additional jobs from. Each dispatching system is different and it will take a while for you to optimise and get a feel for the good areas to sit in.

When you fill in your log book everyday its good practice to annotate which area your job came from along with the time and cost of the fare. You can use this information to build up a picture of what times are good to sit in different areas. In your area perhaps there is a company that sends it's employees to the airport from an industrial estate every Thursday at 15.30 pm for example.

Sharing Your Cab

If you choose to share your cab with another driver you can make a great profit. In theory, this sounds great when you can be earning money while you sleep however there are some common pitfalls I would like to share with you. It is important that you find someone trustworthy, who will not steal from you and work a good amount of hours. I recommend if you choose to share a cab and split the earnings you get the driver to fill out a record of millages and shifts. You can work out an average calculation of how many miles they do and work out what you expect them to earn in that time/distance period.

To drive for someone else, you have to do more hours to make a reasonable profit when working on a 50/50 split. For example for every £5 fare, £2.50 will go to the owner and £2.50 to the driver. As a non owner driver, naturally you would feel more financial pressure and this in my experience leads to vehicles been driven faster increasing the wear and tear on the vehicle. The best arrangements when sharing a cab are to have a trustworthy partner, such as a family member or friend you already know to share the driving with. You could go half on all the costs of the vehicle and keep most of the profit for yourself.

Choosing A Vehicle

When you are choosing a vehicle, you will have to make sure that the vehicle that you intend to purchase complies with the licensing regulations of the council area that you are planning to work in.

Hybrid vehicles that run on a part electric and part fuel engine work very well to save costs on fuel. They use the electrical energy to move at slower speeds around town, only using fuel at higher speeds. You can reduce your fuel bill by choosing as economical a car you can. In some areas, there may be fewer restrictions on the type of vehicle you can license, which means that you could buy an older vehicle very cheaply and run that as your cab. You want your fuel bill to be as low as possible so try to bear this in mind.

Many councils force you to buy a vehicle that is within a certain engine size, fuel type, emission bracket and dimensions. In some areas you can go beyond just being able to take the standard four passengers in a private hire vehicle for example and get a vehicle that can transport five passengers, or even a minibus. Generally speaking the larger your vehicle, the wider your net of fares that you can take.

When buying a car that suits the licensing conditions of the council that you plan to apply for, first you need to phone the council to see if they plan to change the conditions in the near future. I have seen instances in the past where drivers buy a new car, then the council changes their conditions and the driver is left with a car that is not suitable to be licensed and thousands of pounds out of pocket.

Tax

The subject of tax has many new drivers perplexed as to what to do and how to pay your tax bill. There are two was of paying your tax bill. It is very important that when you register you take notes of the dates in which you should submit your tax return by - if you do this late you could end up with a fine.

When you start driving you need to phone HMRC and register as a sole trader. When you register you will be able to enquire about when your tax return is due and you can either calculate this yourself, or pay an accountant to do this for you. Most drivers tend to use an accountant. Keep records of all items that you purchase for your car, expenses and fuel as you will need these business costs recorded in order to reduce your tax bill.

Final Advice

I hope you have enjoyed reading this book and can now make a more informed decision if you want to proceed with taxi or private hire driving as a career. Now you know about some of the costs involved getting into this trade, you should be in a strong position to work most if not all of the financial commitment and have more knowledge on how the industry works. It can be great to set your own hours and work flexibly, on the other hand, it is also a very vulnerable profession to events such as rival companies opening, or having an accident. Try to get friendly with other drivers and in the worst case scenario if you end up off the road, you can ask to drive their car while they are not working.

As a cabbie, you will spend a long time sitting down and in order to stay fit and healthy you should invest in a gym membership and this can be a great way to break up your day and protect yourself from back problems.

You now have all the knowledge to get started and I wish you all the best in this venture should you choose to go ahead. Please don't forget to review this book if you have found it helpful and it has given you beneficial knowledge.

www.ingramcontent.com/pod-product-compliance
Lightning Source LLC
Chambersburg PA
CBHW051404280526
45784CB00007B/3096